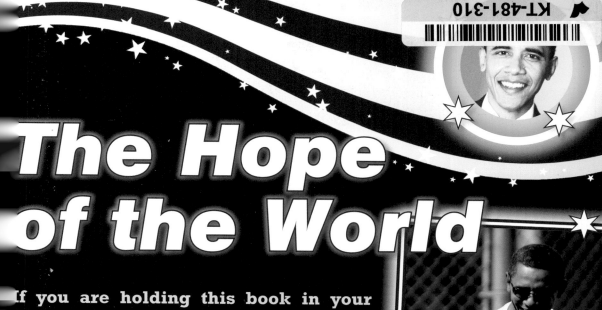

The Hope of the World

If you are holding this book in your hands you are part of the generation of change, the generation that lives in a time of hope, where anything is possible and where belief in your dreams can bring real change.

On 20 January 2009, Barack Obama took office as the 44th president of the United States of America, becoming the first African-American President in history, a country where just fifty years ago he would not have been allowed to vote because of the colour of his skin.

Behind us there stands years of war, global warming, economic difficulties and inequality. Ahead there is the hope of peace, freedom and a world where men and women of different colours, beliefs and religions can live in harmony. A genuine change is taking place and we have a front row seat. One man has stepped forward to bravely lead the world towards our future.

'Barack Obama doesn't represent a colour. He represents change.' Usher

> Barack's name means 'one who is blessed' in Swahili

But who is this man? How has an African-American become the President of a country with a history of some believing they are better than others because of the colour of their skin? How has he overcome the odds against him and what can we expect from this incredible man?

Barack Obama is a man whose dreams and beliefs are important to all of us. In this book we explore those dreams and tell his inspiring story.

Barack was nickna[med]
'Bar' by his late
grandmother

BARACK JNR.

So where is Barack Obama from and what was he like as a kid?

Barack Obama was born on 4 August 1961 in Honolulu, Hawaii. Barack's parents had met at the University of Hawaii where his father, Barack Sr. studied. Barack Sr. was originally from a small village in Kenya and had become the university's first ever student from an African country.

Barack's mother, Ann Dunham, had had a very different background. She had lived in America all of her life, moving from California, Kansas and Texas, to eventually settle with her parents in Hawaii. Ann had been a brilliant student and had been offered a place at the University of Chicago in 1958 when she was only sixteen years old. Her parents thought that she was too young to enrol, so it wasn't until two years later, when the family moved to Hawaii, that she began her university career.

'I am so thrilled. It's an amazing feeling.' Lindsay Lohan

Barack collects *Spider-Man* and *Conan the Barbarian* comics

'...parents shared not
only an improbable love,
they shared an abiding
faith in the possibilities
of this nation. They
would give me an
African name, Barack,
or blessed, believing that
in a tolerant America
your name is no barrier
to success.'

Barack Obama

Ann quickly found herself at ease among her fellow students, including the handsome Barack Sr., joining weekend meetings to discuss politics, world affairs and to listen to jazz. Amazingly, Ann was the only woman in the group. So in their own ways, both of Barack's parents were odd ones out who had to fight for their right to be respected and accepted as equals. No wonder that they found themselves drawn together and on 2 February 1961 the pair married.

All those years ago, it was very unusual and even seen as unacceptable for black and white people to marry. In fact, in many parts of America it would have been illegal for them to have married at all. But Barack Sr. and Ann were happily married on the beautiful Hawaiian island of Maui and Ann was soon to give birth to their son, Barack Obama.

Barack has read every *Harry Potter* book

 ## ON THE MOVE AGAIN

Just a year later Barack Sr. was to leave his wife and son to pursue his academic career at the very prestigious, but very far away, University of Harvard. It was a tough time for Ann and her young son, and she was forced to use food stamps to help support herself (they were a way by which poor families could get access to healthy food), and soon was to seek a divorce from Barack Sr.

Returning to university work and life to support baby Barack it was there, in 1967, that Ann met Lolo Soetoro. Lolo was the manager of an oil company visiting from Indonesia, and they fell deeply in love. Lolo soon proposed and the family of three moved across the ocean to his home city of Jakarta, the capital of Indonesia.

⭐ AN INDONESIAN UPBRINGING

Life in Jakarta was very different from life in Hawaii. At just six years old, the change for Barack was immense. The young boy was to learn a new language and make new friends. At school he learned about the different culture of Indonesia and its religion called Islam.

Despite the many wonders of life in Jakarta, Barack's mother was determined he should eventually live in America, where she felt his best chances for future happiness and success lay. He remembers that 'she had learned … the chasm that separated the life chances of an American from those of an Indonesian. She knew which side of the divide she wanted her child to be on. I was an American, she decided, and my true life lay elsewhere.'

Barack ate dog meat, snake meat, and roasted grasshopper while living in Indonesia

★ LONG SCHOOLDAYS

To succeed in her aim Ann was keen that Barack had the best education possible. Every morning at 4am she would begin teaching him English for three hours, after which he would go on to his school and she would leave for work.

But it wasn't just language and knowledge that Ann wanted to instil in her young son: she wanted to teach him important values. She would say to him, 'if you want to grow into a human being you're going to need some values – honesty, fairness, straight talk and independent judgement.' Meanwhile, his stepfather, Lolo, taught the boy the importance of standing up for yourself and what you believe, showing him how to box and defend himself.

Together, Barack Obama's parents gave their son the best possible start in life. Barack says of his mum, 'she was the kindest, most generous spirit I have ever known … What is best in me I owe to her.'

'If you're walking down the right path and you're willing to keep walking, eventually you'll make progress.'

Barack Obama

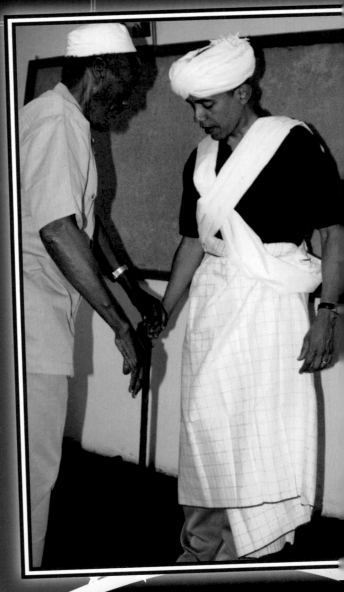

★ BACK TO AMERICA

Given the time and effort Barack devoted to his education it's unsurprising that he soon won a scholarship to study at a school back in Hawaii.

At the age of ten, he flew back to America and moved in with his grandparents in their Hawaiian home, ready for the start of the new school semester. His mother stayed in Indonesia and missed her son desperately but was happy that her dream of Barack's American schooling had begun.

ck was known as
y until university
he asked to be
essed by his full

SETTLING DOWN TO A NEW LIFE

Discovering who you are is one of life's most difficult challenges. For Barack, the journey back to Hawaii was a difficult one. He had already moved so much in his life, leaving his friends behind in Indonesia, and was now in a school where there was only one other black child.

Barack felt pretty isolated and didn't want to just to fit in with the crowd. As he said, 'I was trying to raise myself to be a black man in America, and beyond the given of my appearance, no one around me seemed to know exactly what that meant'. He wanted to understand why and began to study the history of the nation he would come to lead.

'Seeing him could be the one thing that's gonna spark the mind of the young child — whether it be black, Indian, Puerto Rican, Asian — that it's possible for them to achieve that greatness.'

Busta Rhymes

The Long Road to Freedom

UNDERSTANDING THE PAST

With Barack Obama as the most powerful man in the world, it's very difficult to understand how anyone could ever have accepted the idea of slavery – the possibility that someone could be a slave to another person. But it's only in relatively recent times that the unfairness and cruelty of slavery has been recognized.

A NEW NATION

America, before it became the United States of America, was ruled by Britain. It was only a war against the British in 1775 that led to American independence and signalled a break from British rule.

In the next few years the American people set about establishing themselves as a nation. The dollar was introduced as the country's own form of currency and a 'constitution' was drawn up. This document formally set up the system of government and laws that would be followed to the present day.

'I stand here knowing that my story is part of the larger American story that I owe a debt to all those who came before me and that in no other country on earth is my story even possible.'

Barack Obama

17

The new country of America needed a leader, and the honour fell to George Washington, the man who had been so important in the fight for independence.

George Washington: FACT FILE

* George Washington was born in 1732.

* George was the son of a Virginian landowner.

* In early life George worked as a 'planter' – someone who owned a plantation where crops, such as tobacco, were grown and sold. Knowing and loving the land on which he lived was part of his family's heritage.

* George proved to be a formidable leader in the War of Independence with Britain, taking his troops into battle after battle.

* In the country's first election George Washington won 100% of the vote and in 1789 he was sworn in as the first President of America.

BLACK SLAVES

When America began its life many black slaves were imported from West African countries to help build the new country. They worked on the land, like sugar and cotton plantations, for free because they were 'owned' by the white men who bought them. They were also used as domestic servants.

Barack is left-handed – the sixth post-war president to be left-handed

THE NORTH SOUTH DIVIDE

In the 18th century attitudes towards slavery began to change and in 1807 it was made illegal for slaves to be brought into America. Then, in 1833, Great Britain became the first nation to formally abolish and outlaw slavery. However, in the southern parts of America slavery was part of every-day life and black people were just seen as property like a washing machine or a car. Wealthy landowners relied on slavery and knew that without it they wouldn't be able to make their fortunes. So this enormous country soon became divided into two – the North and the South. In the North, the opposition to slavery was at its strongest, and when Abraham Lincoln, the 16th President of the United States, was elected in 1861, his belief that slavery should be ended brought the country to war.

Abraham Lincoln: FACT FILE

* Abraham Lincoln was born into a family of farmers in 1809.

* Abe only received 18 months of schooling and educated himself.

* He was a very tall, strong man.

* As a young man Abe pursued a career as a lawyer and made his mark speaking out against slavery.

* Abe was concerned with bringing peace to his divided country but made enemies of those who wanted to continue keeping slaves.

* Just five days after Abe had brought an end to the Civil War he was assassinated by a man named John Wilkes Booth.

* A martyr to freedom, Abraham Lincoln remains one of the most important figures in American history for his pursuit of equality for all.

A WAR OF FREEDOM

Knowing that Abraham Lincoln wanted to outlaw slavery across America, eleven of the southern states joined forces to form what became known as the Confederacy. Together, they declared their desire to separate from the rest of the country and be free to continue importing slaves. The north of the country likewise joined forces into one group called the Union, led by Abraham Lincoln and his government. A bloody war began, known as the American Civil War, which lasted between 1861 and 1865.

FREEDOM AT LAST

Once the war had broken out, the Union issued an order known as the Emancipation Proclamation. The aim of this was to formally make all slaves free men. As the Union army marched southwards and won more and more battles against the Confederacy, the Proclamation effected more and more men and women. Each day thousands and thousands of slaves were set free. By the end of the war 4 million slaves had become free men and women.

Barack Obama

A LEADING LIGHT

In the century that followed America was to face incredible challenges, each of which would change the nation in countless ways. It experienced a great economic depression that saw many families in poverty and it took part in two world wars but from these terrible events it rose to become the superpower of the world, a nation other countries looked towards for help and for inspiration.

But, closer to home, and beneath the positive image of America there was a continuing problem which could not be ignored: racial inequality.

THE LONG ROAD TO EQUALITY

Despite the abolition of slavery some one hundred years earlier, many states within America continued with practices and laws which segregated, or separated, black and white people, giving white people superior rights.

Black men and women weren't allowed to vote, so weren't allowed to try and change the way their government treated them. Nor were they entitled to the same education as white children. Often they would be refused jobs because of the colour of their skin and in many cases they were victims of violence at the hands of white men. Rather than fight violence with violence, however, the movement that developed in response to this inequality was a peaceful one.

THE POWER OF ONE

The Civil Rights Movement began in earnest in 1955. One day in December, a 42-year-old black woman named Rosa Parks took a bus in Montgomery, Alabama. She paid her fare and sat in an empty seat in the portion of the bus reserved for 'coloured' people. As the bus continued its journey it slowly began to fill up, with the part of the bus reserved for white people becoming completely full. Noticing that some white men were unable to find seats, the bus driver stopped the bus and asked several of the black passengers, including Rosa Parks, to give up their seats. Parks refused. The bus driver called the police and Parks was arrested. She was sent to trial four days later and found guilty of disorderly conduct. But the bravery she had shown sent shockwaves around the country. On the day of her trial some 35,000 leaflets were handed out, asking black men and women to boycott the buses and walk to work. Despite the heavy rain that day, 40,000 people demonstrated their support for Parks by boycotting the bus service. What started as a one-off show of solidarity lasted for 385 days.

'People always say that I didn't give up my seat because I was tired, but that isn't true. I was not tired physically, or no more tired than I usually was at the end of a working day. I was not old, although some people have an image of me as being old then. I was forty-two. No, the only tired I was, was tired of giving in.'

Rosa Parks

Martin Luther King: FACT FILE

* Martin Luther King was born in 1929, the son of a clergyman.

* Martin excelled in school and took a doctoral degree at Boston University.

* Martin became a pastor of a Baptist church in Montgomery, Alabama.

* In 1963 Martin Luther King led 300,000 demonstrators on a march to Washington to highlight inequality, the 'March on Washington for Jobs and Freedom'.

* In 1964 Martin Luther King became the youngest man ever to receive the Nobel Peace Prize. His life was tragically cut short in 1968.

* Martin Luther King gave one of the most famous speeches in history, one that changed our world ...

'I have a dream that one day this nation will rise up and live out the true meaning of its creed: 'We hold these truths to be self-evident, that all men are created equal ... I have a dream that my four little children will one day live in a nation where they will not be judged by the colour of their skin, but by the content of their character ... I have a dream that one day on the red hills of Georgia the sons of former slaves and the sons of former slave owners will be able to sit down together at a table of brotherhood ... Let freedom ring ...'

A NEW VOICE

Dr Martin Luther King became leader of the boycott movement and the success of the protest made him a national figure. The following years saw a growing number of acts of 'civil disobedience' by the American Civil Rights Movement, all of which were aimed at removing the barriers of segregation and racial discrimination. Step by step, freedoms were won, as issues such as education, the right to vote, and freedom from job discrimination were faced head-on.

Just a few years before Barack Obama was born, a major court case ruling took place in America. It ruled that white and black children should be able to go to the same schools. Before that point, schools had been segregated, meaning that kids were forced to go to separate schools according to the colour of their skin. Despite the change to the law, many schools, particularly in the southern parts of America, refused to allow black children through their doors.

OPENING DOORS FOR CHILDREN

Teenagers
who changed the world:

The Little Rock Nine

Can you imagine turning up for your first day at a new school and being confronted by a line of soldiers blocking you from getting in? This is what actually happened to nine young African-American teenagers in 1957.

When President Obama was inaugurated, he invited the Little Rock Nine to the celebrations

So when nine brave teenagers turned up at the all-white Central High School in Little Rock, Arkansas, for their first day of school, the governor of Arkansas ordered soldiers to block them from entering the building. The President, Dwight Eisenhower, had to send in troops to protect the students and ordered the governor to remove the soldiers. But this was only the beginning. The soldiers were replaced by the local police and by crowds of angry white people, mostly made up of parents of the school's white students. The Little Rock Nine, as they came to be known, bravely ignored the taunts and threats from the crowd and stuck it out. Escorted by armed guards, all but one of them attended the school for the entire academic year. During that time they were bullied and spat at, but they never gave in. What they probably didn't realize at the time is that thanks to their bravery they changed the course of American history and opened doors for other children to follow through.

A PRESIDENT FOR CHANGE

John Fitzgerald 'Jack' Kennedy, often referred to as JFK, was born in 1917. He became the 35th President of the United States in 1961, serving almost three years in office before he was mysteriously assassinated. His time as president, although short, was hugely important to the civil rights movement and he remains a very popular figure of history.

TRUE FREEDOM FOR ALL

The young president was instrumental in the progress of America's Civil Rights Movement and when Martin Luther King was imprisoned for civil disobedience in 1960, JFK telephoned King's wife to offer support. Two years later, in 1962, a young man named James Meredith became the first black student to enrol at the University of Mississippi; the university's governor, as well as its white students, tried to prevent Meredith from entering the university but JFK ordered 400 Federal Marshalls and 3,000 troops to ensure that Meredith's right to education was honoured. The following year a similar event took place at the University of Alabama, which prompted JFK to give a national speech on the TV and radio to address the issue of civil rights . . .

'One hundred years of delay have passed since President Lincoln freed the slaves, yet their heirs, their grandsons, are not fully free. They are not yet freed from the bonds of injustice. They are not yet freed from social and economic oppression. And this Nation, for all its hopes and all its boasts, will not be fully free until all its citizens are free.

In this landmark speech JFK promised that he would bring about changes to ensure that 'race has no place in American life or law'. He was true to his word and although he did not live to see the Civil Rights Act of 1964 passed, his work in developing it was of major importance.

★ BARACK'S INSPIRATION

It had been a voyage of discovery for Barack. Learning his country's history had inspired him to take up and continue the hard work of the important figures of the past, to make sure every citizen of the USA had equal rights and to allow every voice to be heard.

He had a long journey to travel but the seeds of expectation, and change, had been sewn in his heart and mind.

A Leader is Born

Having read lots of books and the works of great black American writers and thinkers Barack still refused to do as others did and as he describes, 'play like white boys do'. Still searching for his direction and purpose in life, he let his grades slip and spent hours and hours on the basketball court. As he says, 'I was affected by the problems that I think a lot of young African-American teens have. They feel that they need to rebel against society as a way of proving their blackness. And often, this results in self-destructive behaviour.'

⭐ THE UNIVERSITY OF LIFE

But in 1979 Barack moved to the mainland to take up a full scholarship role at Occidental College in Los Angeles. He found himself among a broad, diverse group of students with the freedom to act however they wanted to.

In his first years at the college Barack didn't apply himself but he was about to experience an incredible moment of revelation. Having listened to some of the challenges his fellow African-American students experienced in their day

Barack plans to install a basketball court in the White House grounds

Barack would have liked to have been an architect if he were not a politician

to day studies he found himself face to face with difficult questions he could no longer ignore. 'Who told you that being honest was a white thing? … that your situation exempted you from being thoughtful or diligent or kind, or that morality had a colour? You've lost your way, brother. Your ideas about yourself – about how you are and who you might become – have grown stunted and narrow and small.'

★ FIRST JOB

Charged with a spirit of purpose, in 1981 Barack sought a transfer from Los Angeles to Columbia College, in the heart of buzzing New York city. There was a drive to his studies that hadn't been there before, and not only did he study hard he also became a community organiser. He wanted to help change things at a grass roots level – starting with the people who shared the pavement with him in New York. In 1983, with no obvious move to be made into political life, he got an office job but the dreams of the Civil Rights Movement and the echo of those who had gone before him fired him towards this goal.

★ TAKING A LEAP

Before long, that siren call had become too strong to ignore and Barack took the brave step of resigning from his well-paid job. He began looking for a job that would enable him to make a difference.

The first step found Barack campaigning for a public interest group and trying to convince students of the importance of recycling but when the campaign had run its course of six months, he found himself 'broke, unemployed and eating soup from a can'. He must have felt pretty adrift, alone and frustrated. But instead of giving up hope he continued to look for the chance that would allow him to fulfil his ambition to bring change.

Then one day he spotted an advert for a black organiser to work for a community development project in the south side of Chicago – the largest African-American community in the USA and a poverty-stricken area. It was a perfect start for Barack and the first step on the path to making a difference.

'We need to steer clear of this poverty of ambition, where people want to drive fancy cars and wear nice clothes and live in nice apartments but don't want to work hard to accomplish these things. Everyone should try to realize their full potential.'

Barack Obama

★ BECOMING A FORCE FOR GOOD

Barack was to find a spiritual home among the disadvantaged people of Chicago's South Side. Here were people and issues that he cared about. And as he later understood, 'once I found an issue enough people cared about, I could take them into action. With enough actions, I could start to build power'. His first major achievement was setting up a jobs centre in one of the city's poorest areas. Doing so would give people the chance to find work and lift themselves into a better life. He succeeded. With the support of the community Barack was able to persuade Harold Washington, the first African-American mayor of Chicago, to open the centre. It was a major achievement.

★ MAKING A DIFFERENCE

The following years would see many similar ventures and it soon became obvious to Barack that the only way that one could achieve serious, lasting good would be through the help of the government. But how would he get that? Mobilising a group of people was one thing, but winning the support of a government was something else. So Barack decided that he would gain the tools he needed by going back to school. He took a place at Harvard Law School, and applied himself with all his energy to gaining the understanding and knowledge he knew would help him. No surprise that he excelled and in 1990 he was elected as the first African-American president of Harvard's 'Law Review' Magazine – a major honour. It was at the cutting edge of law making and had the cleverest minds in the world writing articles for it.

★ MEETING THE FUTURE FIRST LADY

Going to Harvard didn't just bring academic rewards. While working in a summer job at a law firm in Chicago, Barack met Michelle Robinson, the love of his life.

Michelle had grown up in the South Side but had gained degrees from Princeton and Harvard, and now was acting as Barack's mentor. Barack couldn't help but fall for this beautiful, intelligent woman, and after some persistence she agreed to go out with him.

★ WORKING FOR THE POOR

Becoming president of the Law Review could have guaranteed Barack pretty much any job he wanted – and unsurprisingly when he graduated in 1991 he was offered jobs with some top law firms. But instead, his heart directed him back to Chicago where he took a job with a small firm that specialised in civil rights cases. It meant less money and it was less high profile than so many of the jobs he could have had, but it offered the chance to defend the poor of Chicago.

> Barack has his hair cut once a week by his Chicago barber, Zariff, who charges $21

★ BIG LIFE CHANGES

A lot was to happen in the next few years. He was to marry Michelle and take a role teaching students at the Chicago Law School. But one of the most important events was to change everything in his life. Chicago was a place where Barack could get involved in a political sense, so alongside his legal work he decided to run for a seat in the Illinois State Senate. In 1996 he won his first election and the seat for his home district, the relatively poor and disadvantaged area of Hyde Park in the South Side.

Healthcare, the welfare of children and combating crime were all areas that Barack Obama focused on as Senator, supporting positive changes wherever he was able to. It was an early sign of things to come.

⭐ DEMOCRAT OR REPUBLICAN?

Every member of Congress and every president who becomes elected represents a political party. Being a member of a political party is a way of supporting and also developing a particular set of beliefs and values. In the USA there are five parties: the Green Party, the Constitution Party, the Libertarian Party, the Republican Party and the Democratic Party. However, the Republican Party and the Democratic Party are both so large and popular that every single member of Congress comes from one of these two parties. Barack Obama has been a lifelong member of the Democratic Party.

'Americans ... still believe in an America where anything's possible – they just don't think their leaders do.'

Barack Obama

Barack Obama

So how does the government of the USA work?

The USA is a **democracy**, which means 'rule of the people'. In other words, it is the people of the country who get to decide who represents them and leads them. In 2008, the American people used their democratic right to show their overwhelming support for Barack Obama. But how does the government actually work? It's simple!

There are three parts to the US government: the judicial branch, the legislative branch, and the executive branch.

The Judicial

The judicial branch is known as the Supreme Court. It is the most powerful court in the country and is used for making decisions on issues of national importance.

The Legislative

The main body of the government is Congress. It is sometimes described as the legislative branch, which means that it is responsible for introducing and changing laws (legislation). Like in many democratic countries, the Congress is made up of two separate parts – the House of Representatives and the Senate.

The House of Representatives is larger than the Senate and is made up of 435 members. Each member is voted into office by the voters within one of the USA's 435 Congressional Districts. The Senate has 100 members – two people for every one of the 50 states of America. The two separate parts of Congress have different powers but they must act together: laws are passed only when both sides agree with one another.

The Executive

The executive branch is perhaps the best known part of the government, as it is headed up by the President. The President is responsible for enforcing the laws written by Congress, but also has the responsibility of being Commander-in-Chief of the USA's army, navy and airforce.

HEADING FOR CONGRESS

In 1999, and now a father to a little girl, Malia Anna, Barack decided to push his career further. He wanted to become a member of Congress. This would mean becoming involved in issues of national importance rather than those focused solely on the state in which he lived, Illinois.

NEW BEGINNINGS AND DIFFICULT TIMES

Despite the birth of his second daughter, Natasha ('Sasha'), the next two years were difficult ones. He had spent any money he had on the campaign trail and then there was the tragedy of 11 September 2001, when terrorists hijacked passenger planes and flew them into the World Trade Centre in New York. In the aftermath of this dreadful attack a climate of fear and prejudice grew, especially towards Muslims. As Barack said, 'the notion that somebody named Barack Obama could win anything – it just seemed pretty thin.'

FIGHTING AGAINST THE ODDS

But hope did not desert him. After two years of working in the corridors of the Senate, Barack Obama, with an incredible track record behind him, announced that he would be running for the US Senate. This was to be his greatest challenge yet, the most difficult stage of an incredible journey.

The Race for the White House

★ A US SENATOR

Barack Obama announced his intention to run as a candidate for the Senate in January 2004. Despite suggestions that he was aiming too high and the presence of a strong rival candidate from the Republican party, Barack's campaign gathered more and more support as the year went on.

'A good compromise, a good piece of legislation, is like a good sentence; or a good piece of music. Everybody can recognize it. They say, "Huh. It works. It makes sense."'

Barack Obama

'**If** there's a senior citizen somewhere who can't pay for her prescription and has to choose between medicine and the rent, that makes my life poorer, even if it's not my grandmother ... If there's an Arab-American family being rounded up without the benefit of an attorney or due process, that threatens my civil liberties ... I am my brother's keeper, I am my sister's keeper – that makes this country work.'

Barack Obama

⭐ THE KEY SPEAKER

A major boost came in July 2004 when he was asked to give the keynote speech at the Democratic National Convention. This was a major honour to be given and Barack rose to the challenge so successfully that it almost immediately made him a national icon. His healing, hopeful manner won many fans. He spoke of how the country's strength came from its unity, of how its many different ethnic groups made it a richer nation, of how one should aim for a better life for all rather than for a privileged few.

★ A LANDSLIDE VICTORY

Just a few months later voting took place for the Senate and Barack won with 70% of the vote. He was sworn into office in January 2005, and at just 43-years-old, he became one of the youngest members of the Senate as well as the fifth African-American Senator in history.

In office he soon proved that he meant to achieve great things and became involved in a range of issues, working hard for such things as tax cuts to families, more opportunities for early childhood education, and a more open approach to government.

Barack says his worst habit is constantly checking his BlackBerry

Barack Obama

★ BARACK RUNS FOR THE PRESIDENCY

'If we can have a black U.S. President we can have a black James Bond.'
Daniel Craig

On 10 February 2007 Barack announced his intention to run as a candidate in the next presidential election. At the start he was one of many Democratic candidates but soon the field narrowed to include just him and one other candidate, Hillary Clinton. In June, Barack edged ahead of Hillary, the wife of former Democratic President Bill Clinton, and became the main Democratic nominee for the election. His rival from the Republican Party was Senator John McCain.

★ A PRESIDENTIAL CANDIDATE

In August 2008 he officially became the Democratic presidential candidate, and at the National Convention he gave a speech to 84,000 supporters. Around the world a staggering 38 million people watched his speech. He spoke of his own journey, of his parents, of how they 'weren't well-off or well-known, but shared a belief in America,' and of how 'their son could achieve whatever he put his mind to'. He spoke of the American Dream, of how 'through hard work and sacrifice, each of us can pursue our individual dreams but still come together as one family, to ensure the next generation can pursue their dreams as well'.

But he also spoke of what he would do if he were President and recognised that America has a huge impact across the nations of the world. Talking from the heart his speech won him worldwide support.

Barack uses an Apple Mac laptop

★ FROM A TINY SEED A MIGHTY TREE CAN GROW

Barack carries a tiny Madonna and child statue and a bracelet belonging to a soldier in Iraq for good luck

Meanwhile, the number of supporters was growing by the day. What was so remarkable about Barack's campaign was that it began at a grass roots level. Just like the community development projects he had organised in the South Side of Chicago, what began as a word of mouth movement turned into something that millions could believe in and join.

Thousands and thousands of people supported him by giving what they could afford, whether that was $5, $10 or more. And because his campaign used the world wide web to spread the message, more and more people were able to donate and offer support. A change was on its way and an unstoppable tide of public support was carrying Barack towards the election.

A New President

★ PRESIDENT OBAMA

On 4 November 2008, the American general election took place and Barack defeated John McCain. Voters from every corner of the country took part and their votes went towards deciding the outcome. A change had come to America.

★ A FAMILY MAN BECOMES THE LEADER OF A NATION

Although the official inauguration of Barack Obama as the 44th President of the United States of America wasn't to take place until January 2009, it was clear that life for Barack and the Obama family would never be the same. For a start, they were to leave their home in Chicago and move to the White House.

'It took a lot of blood, sweat and tears to get to where we are today, but we have just begun. Today we begin in earnest the work of making sure that the world we leave our children is just a little bit better than the one we inhabit today.'

GRANDMA CARE

Fortunately for Barack, his mother-in-law, Michelle's mother Marian Robinson, would be joining them in their new home. During the campaign Marian had retired from her job so that she could take care of her two grandchildren, 10-year-old Malia and 7-year-old Sasha. She would take them to school and to piano and dance lessons, cook their meals and do her best to keep their lives as normal as possible while the hubbub of the campaign went on around them.

THE FIRST FAMILY

In a speech he gave on Father's Day Barack explained: 'My life revolves around my two girls, and what I think about is what kind of world I'm leaving them. What I've realized is that life doesn't count for much unless you're willing to do your small part to leave our children – all of our children – a better world.'

Barack and Michelle have made it clear that they want to shield their daughters from the media – newspapers, magazines – as much as possible but it's inevitable that they will be seen as role models to a whole generation of children.

Fortunately, with a dad like Barack it's likely that they'll find themselves supported every step of the way through their childhood and teenage years. It's clear that for Barack Obama, no matter how important politics is what really matters is his kids.

Sasha: FACT FILE

Full name:
Natasha
Obama

Birthday:
8 June 2001

Favourite colour:
Pink

Favourite accessory:
Uglydolls

Favourite food:
Fried chicken, macaroni cheese, chocolate chip cookies

Secret Service code name:
'Rosebud'

'The thing about hip-hop [music] today is it's smart, it's insightful. The way they can communicate a complex message in a very short space is remarkable.'

Barack Obama

THE FIRST KIDS

Now that their dad has become President of the USA, Malia, aged 10, and Sasha, aged 7, are set to become two of the world's most famous kids.

But these two have got their feet planted firmly on the ground. Sometimes Malia even has to remind her dad how to act normally … When her friends used to come round to visit her, her dad had a habit of shaking their hands like a politician. So Malia had to explain to him, 'you really don't shake kids' hands that much, you shake adults' hands … you just wave or say hi!'

Just like all dads, Barack can still be embarrassing to his kids at times!

Malia: FACT FILE

Full name:
Malia Ann Obama

Birthday:
4 July 1998 (Malia was born on Independence Day)

Favourite music:
Hannah Montana, The Jonas Brothers

Favourite books:
Stephanie Meyer's *Twilight* saga, the *Harry Potter* books

Favourite colour:
purple

Favourite food:
Ice cream, French toast, tuna salad

Favourite labels:
Biscotti, Tease

Secret Service code name:
'Radiance'

51

★ FAMOUS FRIENDS

Having such a famous dad doesn't come without a few perks and the girls have been able to meet some amazing superstars along the way to the White House. With supporters like Beyoncé, Leonardo di Caprio, George Clooney, Usher, Kanye West and Oprah Winfrey, Barack's campaign trail has introduced the girls to all sorts of people that they wouldn't have otherwise met. And they've even met a lot of their own favourite stars too.

In fact, on the night of their dad's inauguration as President they had one really big surprise waiting for them. Some of their friends from their new school joined them on a treasure hunt around the White House so that they could learn all about its amazing history. But the big shock came at the end … when they opened the last door to find the hidden treasure there in front of them were the Jonas Brothers – Joe, Nick and Kevin! It must have been a dream come true for Malia, who has posters of the Jonas Brothers all over her bedroom wall.

Meanwhile, *Harry Potter* star Daniel Radcliffe has offered to give the girls a private tour of Hogwarts, saying that he'd be honoured to be their personal tour guide. And with *Hannah Montana* star Miley Cyrus inviting the girls to appear in an episode of her show, they must feel like they're living in a dream.

'People think I'm cool – nobody is cooler than my two girls!' **Barack Obama**

★ KEEPING IT REAL

But 'mom-in-chief' Michelle has made it clear that she plans to keep the kids grounded, meaning that they won't get treated differently from any other kids. Although the last few months have been a rollercoaster of excitement, they now need to focus on making new friends and settling in at their new school. Fortunately, both the girls have a lot of interests which means they'll quickly make friends both in and outside of school. Malia loves playing football, dancing and acting, while Sasha loves gymnastics and tap-dancing. Both kids are also musical and take piano lessons.

And despite living in one of the most famous houses on earth, family life will be just as it always has been. But, whereas in the past few years their dad has been away from home a lot, he'll now get to live with them and join them for breakfast and dinner.

★ PUPPY LOVE

One new addition to the house will be the pet puppy that their dad promised them they'd get when they moved into the White House. They haven't yet decided whether to get a labradoodle (a cross between a Labrador and a poodle) or a Portuguese Water Dog. But whichever it is, they're determined that it will be a rescue dog from a shelter that they can give a good home to.

Barack's daughters' ambitions are to go to Yale before becoming an actress (Malia, 10) and to sing and dance (Sasha, 7)

Barack's favourite snacks are chocolate-peanut protein bars and his favourite meal is wife Michelle's shrimp linguini

Barack Obama

★ THE INAUGURATION

When a new president legally comes to power there is a ceremony called an inauguration. It not only sees the transfer of power from one president to the next, but it also is a time of great celebration and a marking of the past.

For Barack it was an incredible moment. With the weight of American history on his shoulders: of American independence, of the end of slavery, of the Civil Rights Movement, Barack read his oath to the nation and made a speech to the world.

And to all those watching tonight from beyond our shores, from parliaments and palaces to those who are huddled around radios in the forgotten corners of the world – our stories are singular, but our destiny is shared, and a new dawn of American leadership is at hand. To those who would tear the world down – we will defeat you. To those who seek peace and security – we support you. And to all those who have wondered if America's beacon still burns as bright – tonight we proved once more that the true strength of our nation comes not from the might of our arms or the scale of our wealth, but from the enduring power of our ideals: democracy, liberty, opportunity and unyielding hope. For that is the true genius of America – that America can change. Our union can be perfected. And what we have already achieved gives us hope for what we can and must achieve tomorrow.'

Barack Obama

'This is a historical evening! We are lucky to be sharing it with each other!'

Madonna

★ RECORD BREAKING CROWDS

A record number of people attended the inauguratio[n] be part of this historic event. A massive concert took pl[ace] in Washington, near the Lincoln Memorial, and the likes [of] Beyoncé, Stevie Wonder, U2 and Mary J. Blige took turn[s] sing.

★ THE STARS COME OUT TO CELEBRATE!

And so began days of celebration including a special ki[ds] music show – the 'We Are the Future' concert. It was [a] star-studded musical extravaganza: Miley Cyrus, the Jon[as] Brothers and Demi Lovato were just some of the stars w[ho] stepped up to show their support for Barack by belting o[ut] their hit songs. Barack and Michelle had front row seats a[nd] smiled along to the great tunes.

A NEW DAY OF HOPE

Meanwhile, around the world people gathered together to celebrate the historic moment. Perhaps you and your family and friends celebrated the occasion? Even if you didn't, you needn't worry as the day will be remembered and celebrated for years to come. The very first act that Barack took as President was to declare 20 January a day of 'reconciliation and renewal', making it a day that we can all celebrate as a day of hope and possibility.

'I fell asleep crying and smiling at the same time. I woke up with mascara running and a smile on my face!' **Beyoncé**

Hope for the World

★ OUR FUTURE

It's impossible for us to know what the coming years will bring for Barack Obama. As the President of the USA the challenges he faces will be tough and he must be all too aware of the responsibilities that rest on his shoulders.

★ OUR HERO

But our hopes lie with Barack: the hopes of a new generation, the hopes of a cleaner, more peaceful world and the hopes for a more equal world. America has chosen the right man for the job.

Barack Obama isn't just the new leader of America; Barack is a hero that everyone, no matter where they live, can believe in.

People of the world - this is our moment. This is our time.'
Barack Obama

CHANGE WE CAN BELIEVE IN
BarackObama.com

'This is the moment when we must come together to save this planet. Let us resolve that we will not leave our children a world where the oceans rise and famine spreads and terrible storms devastate our lands.'

Barack Obama

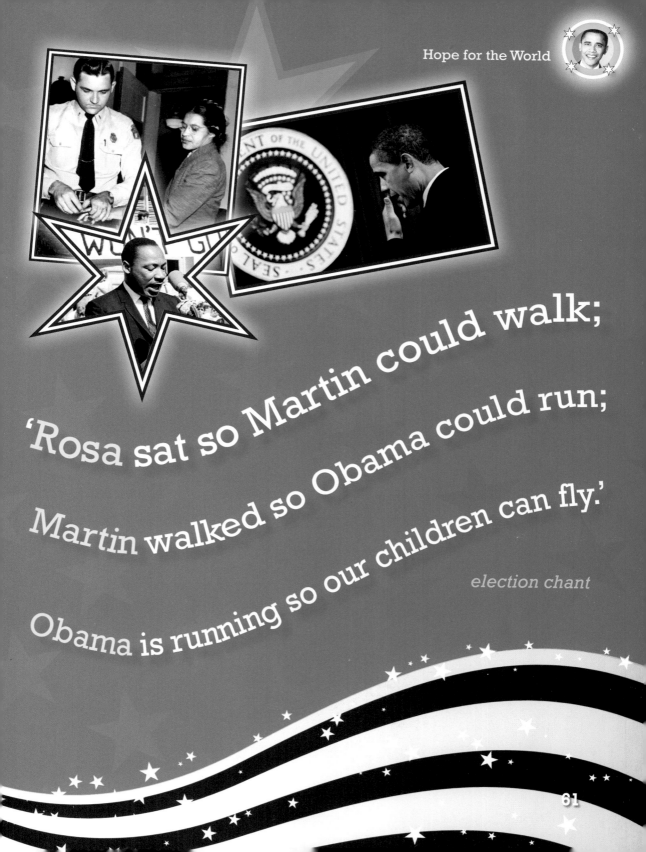

'Rosa sat so Martin could walk;

Martin walked so Obama could run;

Obama is running so our children can fly.'

election chant

Barack Obama

Copyright © Tim Alexander 2009

The right of Tim Alexander to be identified as the author of this work has been asserted in accordance with the Copyright, Designs and Patents Act 1988.

First published in hardback in Great Britain in 2009 by Orion Books
an imprint of the Orion Publishing Group Ltd
Orion House, 5 Upper St Martin's Lane,
London WC2H 9EA
An Hachette UK Company

A CIP catalogue record for this book is available from the British Library.

ISBN: 978 1 4091 1314 0

Printed in Spain by Grupo Cayfo, Impresia Ibérica,S.A.

The Orion Publishing Group's policy is to use papers that are natural, renewable and recyclable and made from wood grown in sustainable forests. The logging and manufacturing processes are expected to conform to the environmental regulations of the country of origin.

Every effort has been made to fulfil requirements with regard to reproducing copyright material. The author and publisher will be glad to rectify any omissions at the earliest opportunity.

www.orionbooks.co.uk

CREDITS

Getty: 3, 4, 6, 7, 21, 23 (left), 24, 25 (left), 27, 34, 35 (bottom), 38, 48, 50 (bottom), 51 (bottom), 52 (top), 54, 56, 57, 60, 61 (bottom), 63

PA Photos: 2, 5, 8, 9, 10, 11, 12, 13, 14, 15, 16, 17, 22, 23 (right), 25 (right), 26 (top), 28, 29, 30, 32, 33, 35 (top), 36, 37, 39, 40, 41, 42, 43, 44, 45, 46, 47, 49, 50 (top), 51 (right), 52 (middle & bottom), 55, 58, 59,61 (right)

Rex: 31, 53

NAACP: 26

Mary Evans Picture Library: 18, 19, 20

Gene Herrick/Associated Press: 61 (top)

ACKNOWLEDGEMENTS

Tim Alexander would like to thank Malcolm Edwards, Daniel Bunyard, Amanda Harris, Rich Carr, Helen Ewing, Andrew Campling, Fiona McIntosh and Jane Sturrock.